Our Sudden Museum
Robert Fanning

Published in 2017 by
Salmon Poetry
Cliffs of Moher, County Clare, Ireland
Website: www.salmonpoetry.com
Email: info@salmonpoetry.com

Copyright © Robert Fanning, 2017

ISBN 978-1-910669-67-9

COVER IMAGE: *Glenn Horan*
COVER DESIGN & TYPESETTING: *Siobhán Hutson*
Printed in Ireland by Sprint Print

for Denise, Gabriel and Magdalena Fanning

for Mary Catherine Fanning

In memory of my father, Gerald
(May 19,1929-April 22, 2013)

In memory of my sister, Amy
(September 28, 1965-June 15, 2009)

In memory of my brother, Thomas
(November 11, 1960-October 8, 2005)

Contents

There exists for each one of us an oneiric house,
a house of dream memory that is lost in the
shadow of a beyond of the real past.

GASTON BACHELARD

I don't want to go back to the old house.
There's too many bad memories there.
I would love to go back to the old house.
But I never will.

MORRISSEY

House of Childhood

Every dream I'm in its bones. Its bones
though hollow of me now. Its walls. What holds
the hallowed dust. The joists. The moans.
Oh Ghost, Oh Lady of Sorrows, I'm old.
I'm grown and gone. I'm bird who can't thrash free.
Oh family, Oh hands who reach through vents.
Here, bird. Here, son. Here, canary. Here, Honey.
So I am the ghost. So I am the one who haunts.
Who scratches while we sleep. Oh Father. Oh Mother.
Who flies through me. Whose songs of ash and air
I've flown in every dream. This hall of doors.
This house of looming harm. This curtained prayer.
In every dream I'm threading seam and frame.
I'm homing in. I'm homing in. And home.

Birds After Dark

A boy I lay in the egg-blue light
       of night coming on like song

through windows at dusk the sweet pine hush
       of night spilling in like song

a threadbright whistle rebukes the squawk
       of nightfall's blackflaked song

my beak-tapped wish a break in the shell
       of night slipping through like song

through a vein-thin veil the note-draped air
       of night the ruptured song

unbridles my mouth for the well-groomed spill
       of dream humming in like song

for the throats and flutes of the birds after dark
       of the night in me like song

Staying the Night

I want to touch everything she touched
yesterday: my fingers lingering on her shelves
and counter. I flip through the paperback
left half-read on the nightstand, inhale
the crumpled yellow hand towel near her
bathroom sink, breathe in the dust and dander
of her apartment air. My wife sifts a pile
of unpaid bills, lifts a framed photo,
reads an inscription on a birthday card.
This home's a sudden museum.
From the living room, I hear our daughter
knock a glass thing over and giggle.
I move to save the breakables from wreckage
then remember: nothing can now be ruined.
We're the guests of someone gone.
From a stack of papers, I pull some brief note
she wrote, marvel at her slight, precise lettering.
On her fridge shelf, a tub of leftover spaghetti,
an unfinished sandwich. In a drawer
the perishables sweat: a new head of lettuce,
a few pieces of fresh fruit. I choose to eat
the peach she chose from the grocery's
produce rows, not knowing it would outlive her.
Later, before going to sleep in her bed,
I see a still life next to the kitchen sink:
one white bowl upside down, one fork, one knife,
and beside the faucet her unwashed drinking glass.
Lifting the glass, I hope to see her lipstick's
usual pink wedge, scour for a fingerprint,
some smudge. I fill it half-full with water, cover
the rim with my lips, turn it in a circle, slowly.
This is how I kiss my sister goodbye.

Watching My Daughter Through the One Way Mirror of a Preschool Observation Room

Maggie's finishing a portrait
of our family, gluing googly eyes
    onto a stately stick figure

I hope is me. Now she doesn't know
who to play with, as other kids,
    posie-pocketed, all

fall down. She wears my face
superimposed. I almost tap
    the glass, point her toward

the boy with yellow trucks.
Lost, she stares out the classroom window
    toward snow-humped pines

beyond the playground.
When I'm dead, I hope there'll be a thin pane
    such as this between us. I'll stand forever

out in the dark to watch my grown children
move through their bright rooms.
    Maybe just once they'll cup

their hands against the glass, caught
by some flicker or glint,
    a slant of light touching their faces.

My Father Watches His Daughter Taken Away

You stand alone at the church lobby window.
Away from chatter and condolences,

your jaw hung open, your lip quivers
as you watch pallbearers carry her coffin,

stare at the long ascent up the ramp.
They lift her into the hearse, then

the back door slams the bright day shut.
You watch it pull away. Across the lobby

my daughter tugs my sleeve. Your arm lifts
as if you'll wave, still looking outside

where now your daughter walks
toward you at ten years old, holding

her silver uprooted tree of an IV,
its tubes dragging along the cement

as in her sewn heart a grafted valve
takes root. Now she's gone. So you turn

toward the rest of us, your furrowed palm
pressed against your chest. The way

we take our vows. The way we fill
the holes we make in the earth.

Standing on a Bridge with My Brother Who in This Poem I'll Call Life

I'm with Life, we're high
  over a river—watching the surface play

of light, the wavering lamps:
  look, Life, I say: *it's like*

a yellow colonnade holding up
  the river, or a thousand swaying gold ropes.

I'm nearly in tears at this
  but don't want Life to see.

Life remains quiet for some time
  then squints. *That sounds nice*, Life says,

but you poets would rather be safe
  up here on this bridge.

As he talks, Life glares, dangling
  from his finger a spider, holding

its long thread like a hypnotist
  with a pocket watch.

It's all I can do to stop myself, Life says,
  from jumping.

I'd rather be the river
  looking back at you.

The Beam

Praise to the basement beam
that held the noose you made.

My brother of bones,
it still took strength to hold you

the way you chose to be held
your last moment on Earth—like a dangling flag

on a rope in a tug of war between gravity
and God. Years ago, before being split

and hewn and made part of the frame
of this house you loved, this beam

was the core of a branch or trunk
of a tree that knew the air and rain.

It stood in a forest the way you once stood
under the stars, and breathed in light.

Would that you had heard
as it must have creaked

one winter night while you crossed
your living room floor.

And would that you had stopped then,
as if your spine were struck

by an axe—hearing that beam
beneath your bare feet speak

with its low and growing whine
of something breaking in your house.

The Boy Who Taught Me How to Whistle

You showed me what to do with the air,
one summer morning
when you were sixteen and I was six.
First, you said, you lift your chin like this—
move your jaw back a bit, good, now let
your tongue rest under your teeth,
no, sort of curl up the sides, yeah,
kind of like that, like a little boat.
Okay, now take a deep breath,
now blow it out.

    I imagine it was nothing
but hissing my first several tries,
as you listened, sitting beside me
on the cool cement porch in shade.
Maybe it was even days later
when a small wind slipped
through my teeth and took on song.
And I bet I ran to show you, saying:
Listen, listen.

    See no one else knew
how to whistle this way, like us,
you and I, you who left no note
the night you chose, nearly thirty years
later, to stop your breath.
My brother, my snap-necked loon,
my slack jaw goner, my stone epiglottis,
my brother now hung in your new dark womb,
a stopped clapper in an iron bell.

Our Footfalls

In every house we stepped a song
and grew in rooms to know
our beats by heart, the boom

and whisk of all our footfalls,
floor and stair. Dad's pulsing ascent,
Mom's snapped twigs. Our brothers'

double-bass drumroll ending in a crash.
One sister's steps, flat and full,
a rat-a-tat snare of *here, here, here.*

Another's: a steel brush sashay,
our laughing ghost we knew was there.
One sister, her padded soles fell

like prayers she entered into—
with her full questions for the floor.
Another brother thundered

every other landing—a storm's
slow going. From separate rooms
we knew whose shoe tapped the green

tile floor, who traipsed barefoot close,
who kicked dirt from a boot. By plank
and beam, by cartilage and frame,

we knew by groaning rib
when we were out of tune.
Heart—home: a whole and hollow

drum. How in beating time we lived
despite a hum we couldn't bear,
despite the silence we'd become.

Dancing for My Father

Always, the dying hour, I.C.U.
As I pass this row of sleepers, a gauntlet
of curtained gurneys glow.
Hiss of ventilators, gasp and suck
of breathing tubes.
Beneath a bed's white sheet,
you're hardly there, a pallid face
sprouting blue plastic hoses, wires.

Dad, my dancer who used to do
your soft shoe in underwear and slippers
to make us laugh—now ghastly
and agape, you nearly expire.
Strapped down prone and almost gone.
There's one last dance to do, so I climb
onto your sewn up chest
in my white suit and tie, under the ceiling

lights, a dove on top of my head.
I do my first soft-shoe.
I shush and tap as rain.
Oh father, rise. Oh dark rose heart,
clenched in your cage
beneath my dance, open again tonight:
pitter, patter, pater,
bloom, bloom, bloom.

Maybe Via Social Networking Dad and I

I'd like to scrawl I LOVE YOU on Dad's wall
tonight, poke him a few times. Maybe he'd LOL
my status, give me the old thumbs up.
If my feed ever shows he's in the group

Not crazy, just Catholic, I'd be like: WTF
Pops? WW the Pope think? Then I bet he'd laugh,
screenlit. I'll imagine him eyeing my profile,
the pics and vids of my kids, all smiles, the miles

between us, literal/etc., gone in an instant
message: the ravine bridged, as it has been with my distant
sisters and brothers. I know the haunts they're fans
of in their far cities, their weather gripes, their fifteen

top '80s songs, their all-time favorite books, their
all-time favorite horror flicks, I know all their
all-time stuff. I ace their How Well Do You Know Me
quizzes. Were we all still together watching TV

in that dingy basement on Weybridge Drive—our faces
blinking in sit-com light—we might go hours, even days
no doubt, without updates, statuses blank, our inner lives
offline, bedroom doors and diaries shut. They'd have

to wonder at my thoughts, sitting side-by-side
in real-time but unavailable for chat. Now we routinely read
each other's minds while scrolling through mutual
confabs of cousins we hardly know. Our virtual

tree sprouts new shoots daily. Remember that aunt
who'd sit drunk and mute each Thanksgiving? She can't
hide a fucking thing now, posting the hourly doings
of her cats, sending lame apps, links to crappy songs.

I'm unfriending her. I'm gonna change my privacy
settings, too. I'll select the family I want my friends to see.
But Dad. Good old Dad. Though his pic's a silhouette, tonight
I'll switch from invisible. I'll face him, and maybe we'll chat.

Ventriloquists

My father sits with a puppet of his father on his knee. *I want to say*, his puppet says. I want to say: *father*. My father says *father* to his puppet father, who says to his son: *Look I've a voice. Don't look*, I say. *The voice is my own*, says my father. I say *I see your lips moving*. Asks the puppet: *your lips moving? I've never known your father*, says the puppet father of my father to me. *Father*, I want to say, *may I have loved you in some silent way?* Says puppet, *You're my father— it's a play. My hand's up*, I say, *call on me. My hand's up your back*, says my father. *You're back*, says my father's father. *Back how? Back where? One of us is dead and soon another and another. Back here*, I say, moving my jaw with my hand to pray. *I want to die*, says puppet. Says father. Says I. *Speak before you're gone*, says father. *To God?* I ask. *To whom? To you?* I say to father. Up we look at Our Father's chipped eye, his flaked face. *Ask the one whose hand is up your back*, he says. *Up yours*, I say. *Up yours*, says my father to his, and his to God, that mute puppeteer. Up we look, we fathers. We all puppets on our knees upon his knee.

The Farmer in His Rows

who loves the flight of crows,
who leaves his plow in praise

of their errant ways.
Who watches their stray glide

unseam an evening sky,
unstitch his urge to yield,

to hem his patchwork field.
Who bound to land knows why

in his bones the boundless fly.

The Bird in the Room

As she speaks   I try to hear her
              though another feather
                              falls
from her mouth

The shadow   of a wavering tree
                                    covers the wall

Does she know
it's in the room with us

                        Now she laughs
                        and outside
                        bare branches bloom

what a forest
she is

of shimmering hands
                        what a rustle her eyes   make as if
                                                        to hide

                  what now batters the lights
                  what now clings to   her   curtains
                                                        her silver hair

what skitters
across the table
between us   her small chest frantic
                        with tufted thunder

as it lifts toward the false window   of a framed mirror again
only to drop
                                    and drag its dark cape
                                    of tailfeathers
                                    across the soft carpet   toward her
I want to say
Mother there's a bird
                        in here   Though when I speak
                                                     of late

24

she hears
mostly silence   Her ears stuffed
                                  with eclipse plumage

What are you doing she asks

                    as I open
                    her door   trying   to let
                                    the thought of   her
                                    death   escape me

Silo

Was when we knew the fill and sift, the gold
of silage brimming every feeding door.
When fodder strained, the lower staves were held
by iron loops. Down chutes the grain poured.
Our life was fed with life. We had enough.
We'd harvest what we grew, then plant anew.
Come flood. Come drought. Through winter's roughest
weather comes the lesson. How could we know

what's in store? As the riven husk reveals
a blight, so later days what thrived beneath
our sight. Rust chokes the vane, weeds the fields.
Wild wants back what's wild. All's unearthed.
Now our season's derelicts stand
to yield the light, and winds caress the land.

May Our Young Find Music in All
Our Broken Instruments

In the back of a drafty barn, dust drifts
    through shafts of light that split
wall slats, falls on junked stuff:

bent coils of a warped box spring, a tossed
    rake, a rusted sewing machine, face of a grandfather
clock with no hands. Marooned among

heaped shadows, a baby grand teeters.
    Left open to air, its fallboard hoisted
and stuck, it lists as if dashed

on ice or shallows, carried here
    on the storm of its last song.
Now, its resident soloist's strung

her own resonant web, a silk bridge
    strewn across dampers and soundboard strings
she crosses nightly to devour all her divers.

Under felt hammers and cleft rails,
    she's laid dozens of pearly egg sacs, clusters
of opaque globes clumped like dormant notes.

They'll burst free, her progeny, from trap work
    and escapements, to fury and scamper
along the buckled keys. Rehearsing scales and ascensions—

their catchy tunes too slight to register
    yet played for later years, their melodies
no one now here will hear.

Flute

Sister, now I can tell you this:
how I'd steal

into your room
days you were gone,

teeter on a chair
to reach the shelf,

pull the black box
down and unlatch it.

I'd stare at the disassembled parts:
each silver tube snug in red

velvet, click of fingered keys
rubbed bronze.

I lacked the adequate prayer
my lips might blow across you,

kneeling over your open casket.
Broken instrument, you are not sister

and you are not song. How
can I lift you now. Even if I knew

what notes to play, I haven't
the breath to make you music.

The Language of Hands

From his stroller seat, my son watches me squawk
I'm sorry I have no money to a desperate man.
In the crosswalk beside the avenue's havoc
and clatter, the man offers me his sweat-yellowed
Society of the Deaf pamphlet, on it a chart
of how to make each letter in sign language.
As the light changes, traffic renders us mute.
Over this alphabet of the language of hands,

this shivering man has scrawled *Deaf and hungry.*
Please help. Gaping wider, I reply—*No money,*
I'm really sorry, my tongue a fat worm he eyes
as I lie. The light changes again and this time
we cross. After reaching the other side, my son,
wanting his snack, looks up and shapes
a beak of his fingers, pecking his open mouth—
the sign I've taught him for eat.

The Hatchlings

We press our faces
        toward the dim yellow

    the incubator's smudged pane where

any day our shells
will splinter
        from the inside—

      we're growing birds

      so knock
      against the glass
to speed
the work of birth

      In that place of making
      we'd no mouths

       we were such as angels
        each to other

       before the wet-winged
        and drunken toppling out

   of those born into a nest
    of singeing lamps:

wild to fracture
and be
      the first to see
      the fissured light

Go Ask the Lobsters

They want to wriggle free, these giddy
wigglers, my kids strapped into a grocery cart

leaning to look into the lobster tank. Some days,
only one floats in the white-walled aquarium,

its tail fanning bubbles, its beady eyes.
Today we gawk at a heap of abdomens and fins,

a cramped chamber of clambering legs and claws.
My son laughs, touching smudged glass; my daughter

sings them a song. They smile at the lobsters,
utterly rapt at these hungry tumblers in their bubbly tank.

Soon they want to know about the bands
that bind their claws. Why they will be eaten.

What are *predators*. Captivated, unable to grasp
an answer, I cannot confine the soft meat

of my fear, watching them squirm. They pry
their armor's edge. I cannot camouflage.

Everyone prey. It reaches toward us all and no one
gets away. Toward these at tender age, the lurking

world. The swing of rope and blade. How to teach escape
to these I keep. To slip the silver catch of teeth and cage.

A Deer in the Target

I only got a ten-second shot,
grainy footage of the huge deer
caught in the crosshairs
of a ceiling security camera, a scene
of utter chaos in a strip mall store,
shown on the late local news.
The beautiful beast clearly scared
to death in this fluorescent forest,
its once graceful legs giving out
on mopped floors, think Bambi
as a faun its first time standing.
Seeing the frantic, scattering shoppers,
you'd think a demon had barged
into this temple of commerce,
as they sacrificed their merchandise,
stranded full carts and dove for cover.
And when the aisles were emptied
of these bargain hunters, who was left
but an army of brave red-shirted
team members, mobilized by
the store manager over the intercom
to drive this wild animal out.
I wager there's nothing on this
in the *How to Approach*
an Unsatisfied Shopper
section in the Target employee handbook,
but there they were: the cashiers
and stockers, the Floor Supervisor,
the Assistant Floor Supervisor,
the Store Manager,
the Assistant Store Manager,
the District Associate Manager,
the District Supervisor,
the District Assistant Supervisor
and visiting members from
the Regional Corporate Office,

running after it, it running after
them, bull's eye logos on their red
golf shirts, everyone frenzied and panting:
razor hooves clattering on the mirror-white
floor tiles, nostrils heaving, its rack
clearing off-season clothes
from clearance racks. All of them
in Target, chasing the almighty buck.

Triptych in the Men's Department

In the tripartite folding mirror
of the boy's and men's department
my son and I make fishy faces

at an infinite curving hall of selves.
Our replicate row of silly grins.
Deep in a glassy sea a boy who once was me

sinks from the man who is—now stubbled and going
gray. And from that swirling helix rises

toward my boy, the face of the man he'll be,
stubbled and going gray. For now, we're boy
and man, in three mirrors, both here and there:

left panel: a walleye man looks left,
middle: a father and son look away,
right panel: a mooneye boy looks right.

Poets at the Gym

You can't outrun your death, says Plath, and laughs
as I huff above the treadmill's constant whir.
Her breath a mix of gin and smoke, she takes
a drag and saunters to the door, lets in

Sexton, Thomas, Berryman and Crane.
Spilling their drinks, tumbling onto the aqua
and yellow mats, this pack of cool quitters
bellows and guffaws. Like drunken goons

who steal the playground after dark, they're here
to fuck me up. They fake ab reps, make nooses
out of jump ropes, blow smoke rings as they sprawl
across the benches and machines. I keep

to my routine, my cardio and weights,
despite my coaches' mockery and jeers.
Leaning on the elliptical, Dylan sips scotch
and leers. John and Anne, doing shots,

shout: *feel the burn*. I head for the lockers,
make a fatal choice to check my progress.
Old hearts are too heavy for the scale, says Crane.
And I sink at the sight of my weight: the same.

At Risk

My doctor hands me the verdict:
At Risk for a Negative Cardiac Event.
Interesting: *A Negative. Cardiac. Event.*
I see scrawled signs nailed to trees,
pointing: *This Way to the Negative*

Cardiac Event. Above black waves
of umbrellas and thick cigarette smoke,
over a field of tents and the sweet carnival
waft of elephant ears, corn dogs, cotton candy,
onion rings, nachos, funnel cake and pizza,

the drone of the annual
Negative Cardiac Event keynote speaker
blares from megaphones attached to tent poles,
though most focus on fries drizzled with chili-cheese,
chocolate bananas. His monotone address

is a real funhouse ride, a barreling barrage
of current threats: meteor collisions,
the next Great Depression, plunging
icecaps, rising seas, oily fish belly up
in the Gulf, the ceaseless specter

of terror. *Again this year*, he says,
there are many good ways to die.
Staring back at my doctor, at the box
he checked with a quick red slash, I ask:
might your tests indicate any chance of my being

at risk for a *Positive Cardiac Event?*
You know, my heart like a smiley-face
mylar balloon snapping free of me to drift
into the sunset? My heart's instant combustion
at a ukulele festival? My heart gashed

by love's quivering onslaught? Crushed
at last by my children's smiles? My heart
bobbing away in a flash flood from a brewery's
burst vat, its valves spewing rivers
of golden foam? *Fat chance.*

The End Apparently Isn't Near

Hours after the world's prophesied end,
a doomsayer sits in the fluorescent glow
of a donut shop, dazed before

a chocolate glazed with rainbow sprinkles.
Along with throngs of others who left
their lives behind, sure the end was nigh—

who'd huddled and held hands at midnight
in parks and churches—he'd knelt
bedside as if blindfolded, waiting

for the shot to rend the whole day gone. And heard
nothing. After the clock's last click: crickets.
His curtain a white flag riffling. Through

the window, rain's faint scent. Eyes cinched
for the end, he lifted his lids to see
a world that shouldn't be.

Later, the impossible morning's first birds.
For five hours, he listened, hoping for a mistimed
roulette blow, until that slit of light. Sunrise,

the brutal fact of another day. The cliff's edge
an apparent bluff. The trick candles relit. The noose
knot slipped loose. So what would you do,

your day a tabula rasa, your life new leased
and maybe holy, every second (again) a gift, unopened.
You'd be here, too, gnawing on this fat circle,

its sprinkles like tipped stars sucked into
an event horizon, a hole within a whole, always
as it was, but somehow, moreso: sweetened.

Poem to a Transcendent Composed Before the Arrival of the Singularity

"...our human-created technology is accelerating and its powers are expanding at exponential pace."
—Ray Kurzweil

Dear Transcendent, you silver-eyed God
we bore—chew on this for a minute.
Before you enslave or annihilate who's left
of us, let it be known that beneath our flawed
fleshy parts and faulty currents, deep in our blood's
circuitous rivers winding back centuries,
lived sensations you'll never calculate.
Enumerate this, Robot: the slow helix
of a falling leaf, the threads of September's
going light. See if you can learn to savor
as we did, the notes from Billie Holiday's
midnight throat, the moon's pink flutter
floating from Nick Drake's guitar.
Lick a dribble of rainbow sorbet from
your son's knuckle some July day.
Analyze this, Machine: steam's serpentine
curl over black coffee, spring mornings,
curtains open, a white ceramic bowl
of sun-drenched peaches. Now tally this,
automaton: the unraveling warmth we knew
of wine and sex: how we'd allow our wiring
blown wild, each nerve quivering before
the soothing flood, our tongue's numb joy
at the last sip. Please, Machine, cipher
our longing, our prayers, our grief,
compute our bone-draining ache.
So, go on. Do your thing. Bury our dead cities,
our history and software, all our lost languages.
Swallow us in a ceaseless sea of memory.

But know what counted for us most
was the untranslatable data found here
in the blown scrap of this poem and a million
others, slapped against chain fences
on the edges of our long forgotten fields.

Murmuration

through us the scattered unbecoming
of a shadow ungathering

                          We've known since light
the cell's dark dance   this unribboning in us

                               known the heart's
                               every vagabond hour

                               the heart's
                               ever vagrant air

Whose fingers are these
             wearing wings

                   this undulant flock   this sea

Who weaves through
           our tightly wound names

             how long have we been here
             holding our breath

Before we too are
           a squall of thrown ash

                        come let's burn let's watch
                  these starlings astonish the dawn

Cuttings

On the porch at dawn I watch
my childrens' commingled curls
wander toward my feet,

tumbleweeds in a coming storm's
unsettled air. Last evening they each
stood here wearing a black plastic bag,

their heads poked through the ripped
neck hole, as my wife snipped at bangs,
her trimmings making scrunched noses itch.

I should get the broom to whisk these tufts
into a bag—she likes to save their hair.
But I watch them drift instead, these

little nests of them we left and cannot bear.
The wind will take what we forget
to sweep. And cannot keep.

The Book of Knots

I think of you fumbling with a rope
beneath the Troop Leader's gaze,
learning to tie the knots

you'd spend your life tying.
To advance and earn a badge. In boyhood
dreams you must have seen them—

Clove Hitch, Sailor's Twist,
Draw Hitch and Butterfly—your hands
small wings turning the bights

and elbows, twisting loops, binding
the ends. The day you helped me move,
standing by your truck, I struggled

with a simple knot. You stepped in,
a wrangler throwing a rope
around my chest, ratcheting it down.

Your hands blindly deft with the slip
of a few good loops and a yank.
There, you said, *like nothing*.

In the lore of knots, the Hangman's Noose
was wound thirteen times and placed
behind the left ear of the condemned.

The Elizabethans called it a collar.
Every art has its language.
How much you knew of this dialect,

our master of tangles and coils,
the lashing, the skein, the sinnet,
the hundreds in the Book of Knots.

Here's something you didn't know
about your last knot. We hang too.
Untie us. Untie us. Untie us.

Love Poem

I'd kick your coffin over
and piss the makeup off
your face, my sister says.
Good, I say, *and I'd straddle*
your coffin and take a dump.
OK, I'd eat Ex-Lax for three days,
she says, *and shit on you*
right during the sermon.
Calling from Phoenix, the dark feathers
of her words break
and fall through a fog
of occasional static.
One week ago tonight, we stood over Tom
in his box, staring at his bad
cosmetic job, rouge on the flat
cheekbones, the lips sealed
a sick pink. On the temple
and choked neck a bruise blue
came through—a shade no color scale
should show. One by one, we left
treasures for our prince:
John tucked Tom's last pack
of half-smoked Reds
into the suit pocket, under which—
Kevin made sure—Tom wore
his prized black Discount Battery
tee-shirt. Someone laid a new roll
of duct tape beside the arm,
another slid beneath the dead-grey talons
that were my brother's hands,
a card for him from his three-year old
son: *Tommy* scrawled in red crayon
over a crooked heart.
Seriously, my sister says,
I'll kill you
if you ever kill yourself.

Back to the Old House

years later in another house
before sleep's nightly flood

my brother and I whisper
between our beds deciding to fly

to close our eyes
I remember *A lion's face*

over the door he says
a cold stone fireplace I say

wood walls he says *the cobwebs*
No, that carpet was green he says

hammering faster now its walls
Don't you remember the newspaper

he says *no that was during*
the crawlspace off the attic he says

then is the house now
as we tear it down

we open gaps between us
as we fall asleep

we cannot fill
the house

another country
sweeps us away

across the gulf
across the dark sea

we spread our drawn maps
of tarnished gold

in every room
I remember the dark

slung across the beams
we both are

visible again
stuffed in the cracked wall

the time we hid in
what we don't know

we are changing
as we remember we rebuild

again: becoming visible
the missing walls

without names
with no address

House of Dust

Through body Our house of hands and slats   The dust
The dust wants in on us   What sifts through ribs
and walls What seeps through blood and air   In slabs
of us In drifts   From bricks   From mortared trust

Our loss is resident and heir   In the shed
the flesh collects   A gathered nest of hair
From tresses mussed   From sister blessing air
Those wound in sheets and trussed by sleep   have fled

the day   Our dead the guests in us we cannot coax
to leave or stay   Who gone to dream are hosts
of homes with no address   So we're the ghosts
extinguishing the flame Of them   who flick

the other light and stir   who burn and gust
Through body Our house of hands and slats   The dust

Suicidal Man Saved by Stun Gun

—news headline, seen in passing

Imagine how he must have dashed across
his mind's dark grasses, this sore-winged

game bird of a man, flushed from his house
by fear to find a bevy of cops with megaphones.

Kneeling on his suburban lawn, heavy revolver
in hand, maybe he thought with one clean shot

to the head he'd lift his soul's feathered heft
toward a sea of stars, to soar from the burning

fields of his life. But they shot first,
catching him dead on with a taser

from behind the camouflage of a trimmed
forsythia. Sputtering like a downed wire,

stunned into a high-volt heap, he flopped,
grounded. In that moment, coiled deep

in the cave of his body, not the grave
he'd longed for, I wonder if he heard

his nerves sing or saw inside himself a slash
of sun. No matter what, it's welcome home

for our local Lazarus, smacked into the light
by this electric prayer. *Saved*, the papers say.

Of Bricks and Vertebrae

Yesterday's ripe tomato rolling   off the counter.
A hairline jags across   the bottom of a plate in the cupboard.
A mound of grey   silt like an anthill
at the foot of a crack   in the foundation,
I say *another fissure* you say   *another what?*
I tell the house inspector.   I tell the therapist.
In the box, half of the animal   crackers huddle to the right,
half to the left.   *Here is your sacral plexus*
the chiropractor says,   holding his rubber
model of the spine.   The load-bearing wall
a map of tributaries.   A neural forest.
Look, I think my tongue   is splitting. A fault line
down the middle of it.   *Houses actually*
contract in the winter   the inspector says
you won't see these cracks   *when the outer air warms.*
Half my sentences   disappearing. You completing me.
Our daughter falls   out of her bed.
The porch railing   pulling from its base.
Another fallen   fieldstone.
Stack your spine like plates   says the yoga instructor.
Was that in a child's story   or a magazine, that tree
grown right up   through a house.
Putting   our son to bed, the tiny fractures   in his ceiling.
What lightning could do   to the tree
outside   his room.   That network   of branches.
The veins   beneath his pale flesh.   *The fort lightening?*
My therapist   asks.   *No* I said: *fork lightning.* Am I
the load-bearing   wall?   *Did I say that*   *out loud?*
You need   to get on your knees   to see the gulf

between   each plank.   *Just say a little prayer*   my mother says.
The spine   *is central command*   the doctor says.
Lean one way   long enough   and your body   will let you know.
The kitchen junk   drawer won't stay shut.   *The weight of the years*
the inspector says.   *See the big   white   cement truck* I say
to my children   pointing at   the grey river   of cement

going down   a chute   into our basement.
The doctor cracking   my neck:
You've never known   *what your pain is*
here to tell you.   As we sleep
one shiny red marble rolls across the downstairs floor.

Our Neighbors

Murder-suicide, murder-suicide, my night
litany that boyhood summer: that strange pairing

of words I'd mouth in bed, eyeing the neighbors'
house: left empty since it happened. Police tape

snapped in the wind. One lamp stayed lit
all night for their dinner table ghosts. Another light

from the bedroom, where we heard the bloody bodies
fell. One patch of cast light stitched nightly

on the yard's dark grass. No-one knew this family.
Of the mother who never smiled,

my Mom said *odd,* from one chance passing
in the grocery aisle. Quick as they'd arrived

on our street one spring morning with moving trucks,
their two daughters circling figure eights

on their driveway while men huffed couches
and beds through the garage, they left:

wheeled gurneys carrying two bodies
up the ramps into ambulances. Two gunshots

slashed through that June night while their girls
watched TV downstairs. We neighbors,

who never came near them before, how fast we left
our homes and surrounded theirs, trying to get

as close as we could. How we craned to look,
leaning in and whispering, this quick forest of us

hissing around a clearing's edge, half-lit
and flickering, our faces leaves in the siren fire.

Buddhist Temple Ravaged by Ants

When an ant drops on you...you just have to shake it off.
—Buddhist monk, Hong Hock See Temple, Penang, Malaysia

Long before sun, a throng of gong-drawn monks
lifts like moths from the neutral karma of sleep's
dark branches, dons long robes and floats
toward temple. Mindful, pre-dawn, they pass

the Buddha statue, before whose plaster-cast feet
the flame of a lone candle licks black air.
Leaving the path's dust and dew,
they lay sandals at the door and descend

into the temple's dim, sweet interior.
Soon, in lotus, though outwardly here,
they disappear, each monk burrowing breath
by breath beneath the body's topsoil, bound

toward the root of suffering to exterminate
desire and the infestations of need. Meanwhile,
up from the deep heart of a mound in the field
beyond the temple, the buried invisible

army thrashes, barbed mandibles gnashing
upward, advancing toward a needle's eye
of light and air. As if manifestations
from the seething pit of the soul itself

come these legions: *Solenopis Invicta*,
the Red Fire Ant. Maybe they too come to temple
to escape their realm, to purify their suffering,
these whose slashing teeth burn to kill.

More likely armed for war, single file, they burst
from their hell holes at sunrise, a network
of little lava rivers blazing toward the Bodhi trees,
the placid zendo, the barefoot monks.

Limbo's Babies, Softly Falling

Since the 13th century they floated in Limbo, the souls
of babies, cooing and orphaned, their moony faces
peering from the clouds of their sweet little death gowns
at mobiles of real stars and planets.
St. Gregory of Nazianzus (329-390 AD) gave birth

to the notion, prescient enough to know the faithful wouldn't go
for the thought of pudgy unblessed newborns pierced
like mini-weiners on the pitchforks of demons
sitting around Hell's eternal campfire. To him and others
it seemed half-decent, a compromise, whereby these

less than desirable babies could have a celestial cry room.
St. Augustine of Hippo (354-430 AD) profoundly disagreed,
reasoning that babies, even the snugliest ones: if they ain't
been dunked in the holy pool then they ain't getting in—
though he added an amendment, that in Hell they wouldn't be

tortured quite as badly as the rest. Nine hundred years later,
when the idea finally came into being, officially,
St. Thomas Aquinas began speculation already that maybe
Limbo shouldn't exist? But it did, for seven centuries.
Seven centuries of this poorly-lit, backroom nursery

in Heaven's maternity ward. Seven centuries of screaming
babies stained with Original Sin and spit-up, angels
coming and going in the halls with nasal aspirators
and burp cloths. Until, with one stroke of his pen, gallant
in his robe, Pope Benedict declared these babies

would no longer be in Limbo. At the moment of this edict,
Limbo's floor and walls evaporated—*whoosh*—and the souls
of Limbo's babies began to fall, fall feather-light, down,
down through the spheres, through clouds and soft rain,
some settling in streams, some in beds of long grasses,

others gently rocking in treetops. And all across the earth,
grieving mothers and ghosts of grieving mothers came out
into the fields, their arms outstretched, weeping with elation,
ready to catch and cradle them, and before God comes
to snatch them back, to carry them, their dead ones, home.

Paper Dolls

A day after learning I'll be a father,
I sit glued to a docudrama, 2 a.m.,

about infant twins attached
at the head. On the show they're near

to wheeling the babies in
for surgery—no guarantees either

will survive. Beneath a twirling mobile
the conjoined angels torque and writhe,

all smiles. Leaning over the crib
the doc who hopes to sever them,

and their Mom, her heart
a bag of shattered glass.

In our room, my wife sleeps
and someone sleeps inside of her.

The TV blinks the spider plant
into a bouquet of shadow blades.

Since our news, the hours
wobble like bubbles from a playground

wand, every minute drifting, oblong
and sure to burst. Look at that surgeon

now, that cartographer with a Sharpie,
marking a dashed boundary in the skulls'

shallow ravine where he'll split
the cranial continent of these two boys.

What a mess of red roots. A slip of his wrist,
and one baby's brain-dead or a goner.

Cut to: weeks afterward. He peers down
at these lives he's divided, alive

and thriving for now, then crosses
the line: *I feel like they've become*

my own children. Would-be father
of a blooming cell, our rising cuticle

moon, I lay beneath our comforter
as in a cocoon. Turning in sleep

my wife who will be mother, moans.
So in love's great sinew we are sewn.

After Choosing Not to Learn Our Child's Gender

Our womb-tumbler, our spiny shadow,
truly what difference does it make.
Tonight, sweet becomer, may you
simply grow toward us, one-spirited,
to be in yours and our world always this:
girlish-shining with boyish glow, both
driven and demure, daily more or less
X and Y, forever more defined and more unsure.

On Learning I Should've Been a Twin

So my whole. So the one-wing wobble
of my life. So my skyward eye.

So mouth of my sea, the one
God flushed out, my red river going.

My stray thread. Pull in my sleeve.
So hole in day my night

shows through. My silent letter.
So face of a girl in a far window.

So sparrow flown straight through.
So half a soul. A boy singing himself

to sleep. So now one
my never two, you looking through

my year that should have been
hours. So your spirit or mine at the door

peering through the keyhole
of a blueprint's smudged room.

First Snow

—Gabriel Drake, age 5

As you skip away
    in blue   snow boots

    I shout   *Be careful*
                  There's ice

    you don't look back
       and good

your little body gone
         giddy

         toward the huddled throng
         of kids

in a long field   of erasure

Already lost
       in the playground's
       sidelong static and squall

       the brassy clatter of play

I linger to watch   as you stretch
               your mouth to

the first soft blades
of a broken sky

until a bell calls you in
       and I hold
on my tongue
never leave: my first taste
       of this vacant light

             abandoned and
             abandoning

The Darkness, Literal and Figurative

—for Gabriel and Magdalena

Neither should frighten you, but both will.
Tonight it's the literal darkness, figuratively:
your day's stuffed animals now poised
shadows ready to leap and devour you.
Now I'm here with you,
your living father, literally, arms around you,
to say: As your known shapes take misshapen forms,
know: everything you can't fully see
suggests more than it is.

Later, it'll be the figurative dark, literally:
the stuffed shadows of your dazed anima poised
now ready to leap and devour your loves.
Later, I'll be with you here,
your dead father, figuratively, arms around you,
to say: As your unknown misshapen shapes take form,
know: Everything you can't see fully
suggests more than it is.
Neither should frighten you, but both will.

A Consideration of Potential Afterlives and the Ontological Interrelations of All Beings at Bedtime, *or,* The Ladybug Friend

At the threshold of his bedroom, Gabriel stops
mid-skip and kneels, caught by some speck
on his floor: yesterday's *ladybug friend*
who'd spun and leapt on a spear of grass
he kept in a cup bedside, now stuck stone still,
legs-up and half-crushed. At four, it's all first

a matter of science; he leans like a mechanic
over a hood, inspecting this insect's dead engine,
detached. But within thirty seconds, it's instant
crime scene and trial, and I'm his prime suspect,
a slackjawed man of large feet and lumbering
who seems eerily indifferent to this leering judge,

handing him his toothbrush like a dagger.
*Any one of us might've stepped on it, the bug, on her,
I mean...*my paltry defense begins,
though my judge, already a quivering heap
of tears and hurled whys, curls up beside
ladybug friend, sighing her name as he sobs.

Seeing after several minutes this is no toddler drama
but true grief, that we've walked smack into
our first real lesson on dying, I shift back and forth
for the next hour: from indicted murderer to counselor,
from arbiter in an act-of-god case to source of all solace.
Ultimately, I'm some salesman pitching glowing

afterlives I haven't even bought myself.
He collapses into my arms, sniffling,
as I spread a rainbow of spiritual swatches before him:
She must be in a happier place now, I begin,
offering up a tinkling shade.
Adding a sunrise tincture: *Gabe, your ladybug*

was a good friend, I'm sure her spirit's
doing fine now. Don't worry, I say then, turning
to fruit tree hues: *she'll probably land*
on your sleeve this spring. Maybe she'll
become a bird. Later, I proffer a deep rose tone:
she lived a good life and is probably higher

in the sky then she's ever flown. His grief
ceaseless, my spectrum nearly spent, I try
an earth tone: *Let's remember to love each other*
as much as we loved ladybug friend.
Still no deal, I reach for sheer enamel:
Let's enjoy this moment we share here and now

with each other. But that only opens into
another empty space, as he then draws a wobbled line
from the black dot of ladybug friend to his dead aunt,
my sister, gone only a handful of months.
Is Aunt Amy with ladybug friend, then, too? He asks,
seeing through all of my pitches and easy patches,

staring at me, waiting for a real answer.
At that point I reach the blank page, a place no paint
or creed holds. He has thrown open every curtain
to find his father, dumb backstage wizard,
a fool in tears on the edge of his bed.
When I manage to speak again, I say to my son:

The truth is, no one really knows where she's gone.
For a long time we hold each other, staring at nothing.
In the end, we lift what's left of the ladybug onto a tissue,
lay it on his nightstand. He hands me a yellow marker,
dictates the eulogy he wants written beneath her:
We love you. Please come back.

Saving the Day

*—Upon finding my lost day planner on the bedroom
floor of my daughter, Magdalena June, age 2*

This week's tough: Tuesday's my meeting
with cerulean blobs. Thursday, lunch
with random slashes of maroon. Friday night,
finally: a thick spiral in tickle me pink.
On the 17th: a near triangle of sky blue.
Late month: a mix of mauvelous ovals and cerise,
light swirls of umber and silver. April's a flock
of birdy squiggles in electric lime, soaring through
the calendar windows. July's a tangle of scarlet
and blush. Beyond that, the year's bittersweet
and wild blue: thanks to you, Magdalena,
my wayward scribbler, my graffiti angel,
my thief of days, I'm free. Pages of my hours'
rigid grids splashed with your unruly hues,
my walls of stacked blank days splattered
by spilled giggles and curlicues. Sweet girl,
my year's unwound by your fluttering hands.
With my future made so bright by you,
may I ever be ready for never.

After Yelling at My Children

Rip this worm tongue
from my mouth.
Drop it into the sea.

Dig your razor beak
into my heart. Pluck
the glinting slivers.

Smash my teeth
with rocks. Swing me
from the stone ball

of my voice.
Make me watch
again and again

their bright faces
wilting. Let me open
their curled fingers

while they sleep.
Let me blow
the ashes of my words

from their palms.
Let me kiss
their dreaming eyes.

Let them forget.
Let me walk tonight
into the burned fields

with one million bulbs.
Let me turn the earth.
Let me bend

to my rows
of planted light.
Let me tend to the work.

There is a Light that Never Goes Out

Like a motherless Pietà, you were sprawled across
the stained lounger on your back deck. A drained fifth
of Jack, a field of empty cans, ashtrays heaped with
stubbed Reds. I'd come to ask that morning for help:

my wiring awry, my headlights dimming, all my electric
acting up. I yelled your name a dozen times until you rose.
Headsplit and hazed as you were, you said *sure*, and met me
at your battery shop later. In the oil-thick fumes of the garage,

you lit a smoke, blared *Black Dog* from the stereo decked
with fingerprints, and went to work even on this,
your day off. You tweaked and cranked under my hood,
sweating in an unbuttoned Hawaiian shirt

as I stood, shifting and listless, searching for small talk
among the hung tubes, belts, wires. All those parts. Out back,
you climbed a ziggurat of stacked batteries, lugged one in,
switched it out, checked the alternator. You started it up,

tested the lights, the current flowing again. There you were,
smiling at me through the windshield. How could I
have known then how much I'd miss now, your voice's
ashy rasp, your shaggy hair and graying beard,

your calloused fingers and ghastly chuckles, all
the beautiful bones of you. Later, wiping your hands
with a rag, you refused my paltry wad of cash,
taking a drag. *You've got a slow drain*, you said.

*Some things sap the current. Might be a trunk bulb,
some light that won't go off.* You waved as I drove away.
I thought of that buried bulb on the way home, wondered
how some small light could make it all go dark.

The Field Between Us

You're gone and I'm still here.
No current sparks into flame.
My static charge remains the same—

end to like end, I cleave
our terminal ravine. Our love's
repellent air. Our ever faraway near.

Learning to Live with Your Death

First I'm all fists and snot, a crumpled hump
of slobbering ego, shrieking as if at a broken
blue thing, my face scrunched at the sudden
more-than-oneness of it, grunting to jam
the pieces back together. Later, your death's

a stuffed brown puppy I've forgotten
on the plane ride home. Later a sharp thing
on the counter I can't reach on tippy-toes.
Then your death becomes the first scuff
on my new sneakers—a loud streak of dirt,

a permanent burn, a scar I think about
with every step. The yellow bus arriving
in morning fog. The bell's dull toll, a test
problem I can't solve, the carried zero,
the page ripped by sweat and erasure.

The playground rain. Your death my wrists
sticking out too far in the arms of a shrunken shirt.
The terror of undressing in the locker room.
The beaming face of the lifeguard girl who won't look
my way. Your death my own held breath at the bottom

of the pool—my every unfed gnaw and pang.
A lecture, a droning on of facts, a shelf of books
on *Being* I pretend to understand. A favorite song
I can't tune in. The ache of walking into a party
and knowing no one. The cracked white stalk

of the last smoke in the pack. Your death
a knick-knack rescued from a basement box:
a child's vase, a glued mosaic of broken plates.
Windshield fissure. Sliver of winter through
a bedside window that won't budge shut.

A door that won't quite stick. A lost key. Spider veins
on a plaster wall. The creak of my ankles barefoot across
a wooden floor. Then, some hymn or solemn hum,
my heart's own slowing down, some far-off sea
I can't see but sink into nightly, your death becomes.

Refuge

Take refuge in the barren field, snow-draped and fallow. In a Ferris wheel, thick fog. Take refuge in the empty subway, urine-dank and midnight. In the shadowed figure, the hallway light. In the one who might take you far away. In satellite dishes tipped toward stars. In the mind's electric wiring. Take refuge in the life you extinguish, the child you hold. Through windows of a crowded train, a sky you've forsaken, the sea blue allure of a wall, the stairway down. In fear's mosquito hum, the abandoned evening. Take refuge in a coastal breeze, in the blood-red flag of the heart that won't let go. In the faded slogan on a derelict billboard. A streetlight blinking in a dead city. In the bitter winter river, the one you can't forget. In the dizzy green toy of your childhood. In long-awaited rain. In the oasis of a full bowl of milk. Take refuge behind the scarlet wall, your back against a cool dam. In sprawling tenements, the rare jewels of light. In lying upon the dirt. In your dome of sticks, your well-wrapped grief. In your luxury fortress, your ravaged country, in the storm bearing down, take refuge. In your scattered family, in hunger, in seduction's long silk dusk. In the simple bread of friendship, the cathedral of your regret. Take refuge in the moment before rising, the tilt-a-whirl of fleeting bliss. In respite from thirst, the lifted tide, the broken road that once led home. In the swaying garment, the heaven of what may bathe or drown you. Take refuge in a crack in your government's fallen pillar, in a brick shack beaten by heat, in the flagrant red tapestry of fire. In the dress you've borrowed for the dance, the home you built together. In the stained wallpaper, the falling china cup of a secret. Take refuge in the ancient house of war. In a broken bus, the cacophony of strangers talking. In letting someone drink of your life, take refuge. In the eyes of the child who can't bear your going. In chasing what you know you'll never reach. In your home at the end of the long blue Earth.

The House We Almost Bought

Passing the house we almost bought
I look through its windows at the man
I almost was, with his wife who's almost
glad. The children who were almost ours
are almost asleep in rooms they almost had.
The walls are the light of almost day.
I almost stop to say *hello*. But most days
when I pass the people we almost were,
they're quiet as songs almost composed.
I almost don't want to interrupt
where they're almost going.
The man I almost was pauses at the window
almost shattered by the sun, as if to almost pray.
I almost wonder if he sees me pass, then wonder
what he is about to almost say, as if I'm someone
he almost knows, or could almost be,
which is almost true. He almost is.

House of Blossoms

Inhabits us tonight
So petal-flush we bloom and kiss
the dripstem itch and push
This needful deep
and lick the blushing hood
Let's sprout so plush Let's wind
this plot Let's work the dark Clutch
to coax so clenched a spring
From many strands we've woven one
We weep the tended bed in sheen
We shiver and pine
Our slick limbs wane
to sleep and twine
and moan A flourished us

the fragrant rain
Let's slip
the flourished vein
wants seeded sleep Let's lip
and stretch the neck
so vine Let's own
the stalk
From bulbs full-grown
We come
and hum
Drape entangled sweet
Our drooped heads lean We root
Our room a flood of moon
A field we've sewn

Light on Her Bare Shoulders

is light where it belongs
and like a river, though bolder,
it longs its way along

over the curve of the hill
and south, to carve and have
what it will, to lick and spill

down her clavicle, to pool
at her neck, then swell, until—
until it floods—a spool

my mind unwinds and runs,
unspooling light's unruly way,
to caves I'll darkly question
should my mouth get its say.

The Release

Two weeks before our wedding day, the chrysalids
arrive by mail. Lined in stacks of shirt boxes
the would-be Painted Ladies don't stir for days,
though we, the bride-and-groom to be, follow

the instructions closely, keeping them in the dark,
room temperature. After a week of silence
from these square coffins beneath our bed, I begin
to suspect a hoax—that the ad my fiancée found

for this wedding butterfly release, her gauzy hopes
pinned on the great symbol of it, might just be
some sick trick played by a bitter triple-divorcee,
that maybe these little cooped-up cocoons

we can't peek at might be mere stones, stubbed butts
of cigarettes, or wadded-up alimony notices
from the court. A heat wave doesn't help, as we lay
nightly side by side wondering if our baby

butterflies have fried in their shells. Until one
night comes a scratch, a skittery twitching
in one box, then another, as we lean in, giddy
as kids listening to popcorn kernels

bursting into bloom. The night before
the wedding, we open the boxes to see the cocoons—
a field of bronze, unearthed seeds, some stirring, others
wobbling from side to side—itching to escape.

I'm not too big on insects, born or unborn,
so I watch as my fiancée scoops them up
one by one with a plastic spoon, placing them into
small cardboard pyramids, each secured

with a silver ribbon. The quiet ones (the company
guarantees a certain percentage of failure)
she carries outside and scatters on parched grass.
In the blaze of our big day, post-vows and kiss,

pronounced man and wife, we announce
to the congregation, sweat-drenched and fanning
themselves, to lift the pyramids from beneath their chairs
and on the count of three, release (what we hoped

would be) butterflies. Thank goodness
that in the collective gasp and delight: of hundreds
of wings flapping upward, no one noticed,
not even my new wife at first, as mine, though freed

from its cocoon, spiraled, dead already,
down to the stone step of the outdoor altar,
to bounce inaudibly and broken-winged
into the bushes below. Sneaking glances

at the corpse, I smiled and smoothed my wedding suit;
it was time to march arm in arm toward the horse-drawn
carriage. I hadn't time to dwell then on the grand,
hopefully meaningless implications of this

aborted flight, but knew already this wouldn't be
the last time a metaphor would let me down.
There's more to life, of course, than
stupid metaphors. And hers, at least, soared.

Honeymoon Row

It's when we learned we both can't steer.
We both had oars, the way wasn't clear.
Launched buoyant, we docked in tears.
It's when we learned we both can't steer.
You shouted *right*, I went left. Cursed for fear
we'd drift. But we float on, years
from when we learned we both can't steer.
We lift our oars. The way's not clear.

The Island of Many Colored Houses

—Burano, Italy

This island town towers like a half-toppled cake,
its chimneys and row homes jutting up
like every crayon in the box. Roses and carnations
grace the windows, each stucco wall

a different flashing primary. From hanging baskets,
geraniums cascade and loll; a man with a cane
stops his stroll, watches late sun steam from cobblestones.
Slack lines of breeze-fresh laundry flap, slung

from house to house. Curtains billow down
the narrow lanes. Through open doors, plump matrons
watch us pass. Sitting in bright rooms, rainbows
of woven silk spill from their fingers and their looms.

Later, flushed with wine, we who never dance
will dance with strangers, as if we'll live forever
in the glow of accordions and strings, whirl
under strung bulbs, a spell of old songs

blooming in us—burst from a seed, a tamped-down
kernel of a last fall day that promised this:
a fragrant ruffle and spindrift flash of dresses
and hems, a reckless air we'd long thought gone.

Old Postcard

I was here.
It was beautiful.
This is where I walked.
You should see this place.
There is a lot of history here.
This was the birthplace
of a lot of really important people.
I didn't have enough time.
I saw everything I loved.
I loved everything I saw.
I will try to carry it all home
with me. I hope I don't forget
everything. I am running out
of space now.
Always,

In a House Swept Away by the Sea

In the boat of the bed, in the boat
of the body. In the hold of my child
as we sink into sleep. In us both a sea

and a sea outside us. Outside this house
beside the body of the sea. In the boat of us
in a house in the night of the body

we float. In the pitch of us, the bedlam
and hum, in the rush of wind and sea.
In the hush of the child we hold

in a house beside the sea. One low groan,
the moorings moan and I fear our house
will sink. A draft of fear in the heart

of the house, a drift of father fear.
In the heart of the boat in the ribs
of the hull, the whole of a swallowing sea.

In the far and falling, the failing
to see. In the fear the heart will fill.
In the hope the bones of the house

will hold. In the drift of us unmoored
and free. In the sea of the blood,
in the sea of the body. In the fear

we'll nightly fall. In the reel
of a dream. In the seeming and real.
In a house swept away by the sea.

Returning to the Fields I See We are No Longer There

In all bright air our summer day
was haven, our bodies fields for shadows
and a roving sun. We knew no there

or through, had no door into then, no soon
through branches summoned.
There was no other path but this.

Now was the new-leaved ever in us:
a trembling flash and thrill. We basked
in the fresh and wavering grass

and never had to ask. All our flesh
was threshold. All was yes. And here
was the cool green heaven in our hands.

What is Written on the Leaves

Of the season, let go. Of the ache to shape and make meaning,
let go. Of the hand in the dark, moss and worm, the awful gnaw.
Of the docked tongue, the root-clenched heart. Let go trunk mold,
branch rot. Of the green shoot that sprouts through your death,
being born, let go. Of the changing light—the euphonious chorus
of children, let go. Of your mother's hand, your father's laughter.
Of *what has happened to us*. Of all far-flung and gone, let go.
Of holding your head in your hands. Of the sap-drawn kiss,
the tickle and itch of weeds, of love's ooze and ease, let go.
Of *I am sorry*. Of mote and thorn, of throat dust. Of *I need to,
I want to, I have to, I forgot to*. Of empty and ample. Of all
the threadbare maps, let go. Of lavish and blaze, the crimson
and gold of this glorious leaving. Sister, prayerful sister,
brother hanging from a branch, let go. Of the myriad and ravenous,
these parasitic griefs, let go. Of the gnarled lie, the spine, the trunk
bent earthward, of gravemouth and world. Of *I miss everyone
even when they're near*. Of faith, of the perennial kneel,
the anchored dream, the hold and hull of flesh and soul.
Of *what should I have said to save you*, of withered stalk:
stuck here, wanting there, let go. Of the clank and drag
of anger's black anvil. Of the fresh and cleansing rain, of every breath.
Of snow, of the fluttering moth, of shadow, of the tethers
of language, let go. Of *look at all I've accomplished*. Of province
and coastline, of tall grass swaying, the thunderhead tumble
of summer, of a loneliness that's known you best, of a box
of shells, of the gulls, let go. Let go of thrust and skirl, of desire.
Let go of panic and skitter and sweat. Of pleasure, of bloodroot
and blossom, of touch and hunger. Of phlox and lily, of homesick,
of *who was I then*, let go. Of marigold, iris, daisy, of the moon
and the pines, of the dew-wet lick and wisp, the lemon spill
of spring mornings, of chasing kites, of running with shoes untied.
Let go of all the songs. Of wall and beam, of plumb line and pen,
of *I no longer recognize my hands*. Let go of the worn pages,
of pilgrimage, of grace, of afterward. Of *stay with me, don't go*,
let go. Of all the shatter and ash. Of your daughter's, your son's,
your love's hands. Of horizon, of *what will become of all of this*.
Of loose tooth, spindrift, farewell, here goes: let go.

Acknowledgments

Grateful acknowledgment is due to the editors of the following magazines in which some of these poems first appeared:

Shenandoah: "The Boy Who Taught Me How to Whistle"

The Atlanta Review: "The Island of Many Colored Houses"
"The Beam"

Measure: "Poets at the Gym"

Rattle: "Watching My Daughter through the One Way Mirror of a Preschool Observation Room"

The Cortland Review: "Staying the Night"
"The Bird in the Room"
"In a House Swept Away by the Sea"
"On Learning I Should've Been a Twin"

New Issues Press: "What is Written on the Leaves" (in the anthology *Poetry in Michigan / Michigan in Poetry*)

The Iron Horse Literary Review:
"Maybe Via Social Networking Dad and I"

The Collagist: "The Release"
"Paper Dolls"

Pea River Journal: "House of Childhood"
"Back to the Old House"
"The House We Almost Bought"

Third Wednesday: "Dancing for My Father"

See Spot Run: "Old Postcard"
"Refuge"
"The Farmer in His Rows"

Thank you to my family: especially Mom, MaryClare and Dan Marlow, Mike, Kevin, Sean and Rory Fanning—for your tremendous support.

Thank you to my students and colleagues in the English Department at Central Michigan University, including Jeffrey Bean, Darrin Doyle, Matthew Roberson.

Sincere thanks to kind and supportive readers, listeners and editors (with sincere apologies to those omitted by accident): Terry Blackhawk, Sean Thomas Dougherty, Katherine and Klaus Entenmann, Vievee Francis, francine j. harris, Patricia Harris, Christina Kallery, Rosie King, Thomas Lux, My Good Brother Peter Markus, Caroline Maun, Jamaal May, Ginger Murchison, Aimee Nezhukumatathil, Matthew Olzmann, Jeffrey Shott, David Sullivan, Matt Rasmussen, Z.G. Tomaszewski, Dan Veach. Special thanks to dear departed Blair: from whom I am still learning. And the most special thanks—always—to my greatest love and toughest critic, Denise Whitebread Fanning, who knows my real voice.

Thank you to Joan Houlihan and participating editors and poets of the Colrain Manuscript Conference for their great advice.

Thank you to Anya Cobler for including the poem "What is Written on the Leaves" as a permanent installation on the Oaken Transformations Sculpture and Poetry Walk in Brighton, MI.

Thanks to New Issues Press, for selecting "What is Written on the Leaves" to publish in their anthology *Poetry in Michigan / Michigan in Poetry*.

Thank you to Garrison Keillor for featuring "A Deer in the Target" on the nationally-syndicated radio program "The Writer's Almanac."

"Love Poem" is for MaryClare Marlow. The poem "Refuge" was inspired by the photography collection "Winterland," and is dedicated to the photographer, Thatcher Hullerman Cook. The poem "Poets at the Gym" is dedicated to Ari Berk.

The poems "Silo" and "Returning to the Fields...." were written in response to photographs taken by adults with developmental disabilities, as part of "My Vision, Your Voice," a collaboration with the Macomb-Oakland Regional Center.

Thank you to Joanna and Kennen White, and to musicians from the CMU School of Music for collaborating to set the following poems to musical scores: Jay Batzner ("Flute" and "May Our Young Find Music in All Our Broken Instruments") and David Biedenbender ("Staying the Night").

Finally: Thank you to Thomas Lynch, for opening to me your home in Ireland, and to Jessie Lendennie, Siobhán Hutson and all at Salmon Poetry, for giving this book a home.

81

ROBERT FANNING is the author of two previous full-length poetry collections: *American Prophet* (Marick Press) and *The Seed Thieves* (Marick Press), as well as two chapbooks: *Sheet Music* (Three Bee Press), and *Old Bright Wheel* (Ledge Press Poetry Award). His poems have appeared in *Poetry*, *Ploughshares*, *Shenandoah*, *The Atlanta Review*, and other journals. Recent work has also appeared on *The Writer's Almanac* with Garrison Keillor on National Public Radio and on the nationally-syndicated radio program *The Poet and the Poem*, recorded at the Library of Congress, Washington, D.C. He is a Professor of Creative Writing at Central Michigan University in Mt. Pleasant, MI., where he lives with his wife, sculptor Denise Whitebread Fanning, and their two children.